MULTIPLE CHOICE QUESTIONS

GOODS & SERVICES TAX

Dedicated to My Beloved Parents & Guru's

PREAMBLE

It gives me an indeed a great pleasure and privilege to offer a book titled 'GOODS AND SERVICES TAX- Multiple Choice Questions' to our young, dynamic and beloved readers and students.

In the recent past Management has emerged as a commanding stance for the entire corporate world where the business world is more and more competitive. Now the corporate cannot afford only to work out plans or strategies without its ground reality.

I express my deep gratitude towards our Dr. D. Y. Patil Vidyapeeth's Chancellor Dr. P. D. Patil, Vice-Chancellor Dr. N. J. Pawar, Secretary Dr. Somnath Patil, Trustee Dr. (Mrs) Smita Patil, Dean & Director Faculty of Management Dr. Chetan Chaudhari, for his timely guidance and motivation for completion and writing of this book. A successful achiever has to work on all possible parameters to maintain work life balance. One important parameter is 'time' and 'Time management'. My parent's motivation and support kept reminding and encourage me about the timely completion of this book.

My students, colleagues and readers have always referred, appreciated and recommended writings. They are the ultimate 'value drivers' in this outcome and achievement. Their 'value expectations' assess my performance towards quality of work. As an author my heartfelt indebtedness to all of them is perpetual.

At the end, how do I forget the 'almighty' who reminds me of my inner strength!

Readers are most welcome to help me to improve the contents and presentation of this book. Let 'Creative Thinking' continue endlessly, so that the purpose and quality of book improves perpetually.

Dr. Babasaheb Jadhav
Associate Professor
Dr. D. Y. Patil Vidyapeeth's
Global Business School & Research Centre, Pune, Maharashtra, India

ABOUT THE BOOK

Book encourages a trend of professionals towards the betterment of Management. The theoretical concepts and choice questions included are the state-of-the-art direction and position on the challenging issues of management and decision making.

This well-known book helps the readers and students to develop the insight and analytical and decision making skills required for today's managers in day to day business activities.

Students also learn how the real world managers design, implement and use management strategies in decision making, tools and techniques for the implementation of business strategies and achievement of Organisational goals, stability and growth.

Salient features of book are:
- Learner Friendly Approach
- Wide Coverage
- Presentation of Text with Diagrams, Figures and Images.
- Guided with Examples
- Organized Presentation
- Lucid and Simple Language

ABOUT THE AUTHOR

Prof. (Dr.) Babasaheb Jadhav is an Associate Professor in the area of Financial Management and International Business Management at Dr. D. Y. Patil Vidyapeeth's, Global Business School and Research Centre, Pune, Maharashtra, India.

He has more than 10 years of experience in Industry, Research and Academics. He has completed his PhD from Savitribai Phule Pune University (SPPU) Formerly Pune University in Financial Management. He has a Dual Master's Degree in Business Administration (MBA in Financial Management and International Business Management) and Bachelor's Degree in Business Administration (BBA in Financial Management).

He has in his credit ongoing Funded Research Projects, 7 Books, more than 50 Research Papers in various National and International Scopus, UGC Care Indexed Journal's with high Impact Factors, 4 Case Studies in reputed International Journals with high Impact Factors and one of his case study was published by Case Centre, UK and 4 Articles in reputed Magazines as well as National Newspapers.

He is also working as Editorial Board Member and Advisory Board Member for various Management Journals or Conferences. He has invited as resource person for Guest Lectures, Workshops and Conferences.

His areas of interest and research are Financial Management, Taxation, Economics, General Management and International Business Management.

GOODS AND SERVICES TAX

SYLLABUS

1) Introduction, Overview and Evolution of GST:
    1.1 Indirect tax structure in India
    1.2 Introduction to Goods and Service Tax (GST) - Key Concepts
    1.3 Phases of GST, GST Council
    1.4 Taxes under GST, Cess

2) Registration under GST:
    1.1 Threshold for Registration
    1.2 Regular Tax Payer
    1.3 Composition Tax Payer
    1.4 Casual Taxable Person
    1.5 Non-Resident Taxable Person
    1.6 Unique Identification Number
    1.7 Registration Number Format

3) Supply under GST and Valuation of Supply:
    1.1 Supply
    1.2 Place of Supply, Interstate Supply, Export of Service, Export of Goods, Import of Service, Import of Goods
    1.3 Valuation of Supply (Numerical on valuation and calculation of tax)

4) Input Tax Credit under GST & Returns:
    1.1 Input tax credit process
    1.2 Negative List for Input tax credit
    1.3 Input Tax Credit Utilization and Input Tax Credit Reversal
    1.4 Types of GST returns and their due dates, late filing, late fee and interest

5) Custom Duty and Indirect Taxation:
    1.1 Definitions of certain terms relating to the custom act, custom tariff act, Levy and types of custom duties
    1.2 Indirect taxation applicable to few commodities levied by either Central or State Government.

MULTIPLE CHOICE QUESTIONS

Unit 1

INTRODUCTION, OVERVIEW AND EVOLUTION OF GST

1) Goods and Services Tax (GST) is an indirect tax levied in India on the sale of:
   a) Products and services
   b) Goods and services
   c) Equipments and services
   d) Manufacturing goods
2) Goods and services tax are divided into _______ slabs.
   a) 2
   b) 3
   c) 4
   d) 5
3) GST came into effect from:
   a) 30th June 2017
   b) 31st July 2017
   c) 1st July 2017
   d) 10th July 2017
4) The President of India approved the Constitution Amendment Bill for Goods and Services Tax (GST) on:
   a) 8th September 2016
   b) 1st July 2017
   c) 31st March 2017
   d) 31st December 2016
5) The threshold for levy of GST is a turnover of Rs.:
   a) 50 lakhs
   b) 90 lakhs
   c) 1 crores
   d) 1 million
6) For a taxpayer who conducts business in a northeastern State of India the threshold is Rs.:
   a) 1,00,000
   b) 5,00,000
   c) 10,00,000

   d) 15,00,000
7) The Amendment Bill suggests levy of GST on all goods and services, except:
   a) Alcohol
   b) Gold
   c) Electronic goods
   d) Consumer goods
8) The tax is levied as Dual GST by the Centre:
   a) SGST
   b) CGST
   c) UTGST
   d) IGST
9) The tax is levied as Dual GST by the State:
   a) SGST
   b) CGST
   c) UTGST
   d) IGST
10) The tax is levied as Dual GST by the Union Territories:
   a) SGST
   b) CGST
   c) UTGST
   d) IGST
11) The tax is levied as Dual GST by the Centre as inter-state sale:
   a) SGST
   b) CGST
   c) UTGST
   d) IGST
12) GSTN stands for:
   a) Goods and Services Tax Number
   b) Goods and Services Tax Network
   c) Goods and Services Total Number
   d) Goods and Services Total Network
13) Goods and Services Tax Network (GSTN) was set up as a private company by the Government under Section 25 of the Companies Act 1956:
   a) 2013
   b) 2014
   c) 2015
   d) 2016
14) GST is applicable on the __________ of goods and services:
   a) Production
   b) Sale

c) Supply

d) Purchases

15) Taxpayers with an aggregate turnover in a financial year would be exempt from tax up to Rs. :

a) 10 lakhs

b) 20 lakhs

c) 30 lakhs

d) 40 lakhs

16) Composition levy in case of restaurants is:

a) 1.5%

b) 2.5%

c) 3.5%

d) 4.5%

17) HSN stands for:

a) Harmonized System of Nomenclature

b) Harmonized System of Network

c) Harmonized Structure of Nomenclature

d) Harmonized Structure of Network

18) Taxpayers whose turnover is above Rs. 1.5 crores but below Rs. 5 crores shall use _______ digit HSN code:

a) 1

b) 2

c) 3

d) 4

19) Taxpayers whose turnover is Rs. 5 crores and above shall use _________ digit HSN code:

a) 1

b) 2

c) 3

d) 4

20) SPV stands for:

a) Special Purpose Vehicle

b) Special Purpose Van

c) Specialized Purpose Vehicle

d) Specialized Purpose Van

21) The Goods and Services Tax was launched at midnight on 1st July 2017 by:

a) Pranab Mukharjee and Arun Jetly

b) Pranab Mukharjee and Narendra Modi

c) Narendra Modi and Arun Jetly

d) Pranab Mukharjee and Urjit Patel

22) There are around ________ countries in the world that have GST in place.

a) 140
b) 150
c) 160
d) 170

23) PM Narendra Modi called GST a:
a) Good and Simple Tax
b) Good and Short Tax
c) Great and Simple Tax
d) Good and Sweet Tax

24) The tax launched under the banner of 'One Nation One Tax' is:
a) Income tax
b) Indirect tax
c) GST
d) Custom duty

25) Transfer of Property Act:
a) 1882
b) 1992
c) 1956
d) 1961

26) Information Technology Act:
a) 1991
b) 1999
c) 2000
d) 2001

27) Indian Contract Act:
a) 1872
b) 1972
c) 1891
d) 1991

28) Under GST board means:
a) SEBI
b) CBEC
c) RBI
d) EXIM

29) GST Act:
a) 2015
b) 2016
c) 2017
d) 2018

30) Supply of goods or services or both which is not leviable to tax under this Act is:

a) Taxable supply
b) Non taxable supply
c) Exempted supply
d) Free supply

31) There are ______ States and ________ Union Territories in India.
a) 29 and 7
b) 30 and 6
c) 31 and 8
d) 28 and 5

32) The constitution of GST council consist of:
a) 29 members
b) 30 members
c) 31 members
d) 32 members

33) The chairman of GST council is:
a) President
b) Prime Minister
c) Finance Minister
d) RBI Governor

34) The chairman of GST council is:
a) Pranab Maukharjee
b) Narendra Modi
c) Arun Jetly
d) Urjit Patel

35) The Central Goods and Services Tax bill, Integrated Goods and Services Tax bill, Union Territories Goods and Services Tax bill and Goods and Services Tax bill have been passed by the Lok Sabha on
a) 29th March 2017
b) 31st March 2017
c) 30th June 2017
d) 1st July 2017

36) The Central Goods and Services Tax bill, Integrated Goods and Services Tax bill, Union Territories Goods and Services Tax bill and Goods and Services Tax bill have been passed by the Rajya Sabha on
a) 6th April 2017
b) 30th June 2017
c) 1st July 2017
d) 10th July 2017

37) GST on gold is:
a) 2%

b) 3%

c) 4%

d) 5%

38) Education cess is:

a) 1%

b) 2%

c) 3%

d) 4%

39) Swachh Bharat cess is:

a) 0.5%

b) 1%

c) 2%

d) 3%

40) The tax rate _____ % with input tax credit is being imposed on Jewelers.

a) 10%

b) 12.5%

c) 15%

d) 20%

41) Special additional duty of custom on goods imported is:

a) 1%

b) 2%

c) 3%

d) 4%

42) As per the Goods and Services Tax (Compensation to State) Act 2017, GST compensation cess would be levied for a period of _____ years from GST implementation.

a) 3

b) 4

c) 5

d) 6

43) GST cess is a compensation cess levied under section _____ of The Goods and Services Tax (Compensation to State) Act 2017.

a) 8

b) 10

c) 12

d) 15

44) GST rates on _________ items were approved at the 14th GST Council meeting held at Srinagar on 18th and 19th of May 2017.

a) 1055

b) 1149

c) 1211

d) 1299

45) The Central Board of Excise and Customs constituted under the Central Boards of Revenue Act:
   a) 1956
   b) 1961
   c) 1963
   d) 1974

46) UIN stands for:
   a) Unique Identity Number
   b) Unique Identity Nomenclature
   c) Universal Identity Number
   d) Universal Identity Nomenclature

47) Motor vehicle act (E way bill):
   a) 1980
   b) 1988
   c) 1995
   d) 2000

48) In relation to a person, shall mean receipt of goods or services or both whether by purchase, acquisition or any other means with or without consideration is:
   a) Outward supply
   b) Output supply
   c) Inward supply
   d) Input supply

49) ISD stands for:
   a) Input Service Distributor
   b) Inward Service Distributor
   c) Input Service Department
   d) Inward Service Department

50) VMI stands for:
   a) Vendor Managed Input
   b) Vendor Managed Inventory
   c) Vendor Machine Inventory
   d) Vendor Machine Input

Answer Keys:

1	B	11	D	21	B	31	A	41	D
2	D	12	B	22	C	32	C	42	E
3	C	13	A	23	A	33	C	43	A
4	A	14	C	24	C	34	C	44	C
5	D	15	C	25	A	35	A	45	C
6	B	16	B	26	C	36	A	46	A
7	A	17	A	27	A	37	B	47	B
8	B	18	B	28	B	38	B	48	C
9	A	19	D	29	C	39	A	49	A
10	C	20	A	30	B	40	B	50	B

Unit 2

REGISTRATION UNDER GST

1. Small businesses having all India aggregate turnovers below Rs. _________ need not register.
   a) 10 lakhs
   b) 20 lakhs
   c) 30 lakhs
   d) 40 lakhs
2. GSTIN stands for:
   a) Goods and Services Tax Identification Network
   b) Goods and Services Tax Identification Norms
   c) Goods and Services Tax Identification Nature
   d) Goods and Services Tax Identification Number
3. GSTIN is having:
   a) 10 digits
   b) 12 digits
   c) 15 digits
   d) 18 digits
4. The first 2 digits of the GSTIN are for:
   a) State code
   b) PAN number
   c) Entity code
   d) Check sum number
5. The middle 10 digits of the GSTIN are for:
   a) State code
   b) PAN number
   c) Entity code
   d) Check sum number
6. The second last 2 digits of the GSTIN are for:
   a) State code
   b) PAN number
   c) Entity code
   d) Check sum number
7. The last digit of the GSTIN is the:
   a) State code
   b) PAN number
   c) Entity code
   d) Check sum number
8. A person is one who has a registered business in some State in India, but wants to effect supplies from some other State in which he is not having any fixed place of business is a:

    a) Taxable person
    b) Casual taxable person
    c) Exempted person
    d) Tax free person

9. A total of ______ forms/formats have been prescribed in the GST registration rules.
    a) 10
    b) 20
    c) 30
    d) 40

10. Proper Officer has to cancel the registration within ______ days from the date of application or the date of reply to notice.
    a) 10
    b) 20
    c) 30
    d) 40

11. Taxpayers with an aggregate turnover of Rs. _________ **lakhs** would be exempted from tax.
    a) 10
    b) 20
    c) 30
    d) 40

12. The tax payer from North Indian states and Sikkim, the exemption would be:
    a) 10
    b) 20
    c) 30
    d) 40

13. Any person with the aggregate turnover not exceeding Rs. ______ lakhs shall be eligible to pay tax by composition scheme.
    a) 25
    b) 50
    c) 75
    d) 100

14. Any person with the aggregate turnover not exceeding Rs. ______ lakhs for North Eastern States shall be eligible to pay tax by composition scheme.
    a) 25
    b) 50
    c) 75
    d) 100

15. Provisions for tax deduction at source shall apply as notified under the act if the value of supply under a contract exceeds Rs.:
    a) 2.5 lakhs

b) 5 lakhs
c) 7.5 lakhs
d) 10 lakhs

16. The taxpayers who have turnover below 1.5 crores:
    a) HSN code is not mandatory
    b) HSN code 2 digit is mandatory
    c) HSN code 4 digit is mandatory
    d) HSN code 8 digit is mandatory

17. The taxpayers who have turnover limit 1.5 crores to 5 crores:
    a) HSN code is not mandatory
    b) HSN code 2 digit is mandatory
    c) HSN code 4 digit is mandatory
    d) HSN code 8 digit is mandatory

18. The taxpayers who have turnover limit above 5 crores:
    a) HSN code is not mandatory
    b) HSN code 2 digit is mandatory
    c) HSN code 4 digit is mandatory
    d) HSN code 8 digit is mandatory

19. The taxpayers who have export business only:
    a) HSN code is not mandatory
    b) HSN code 2 digit is mandatory
    c) HSN code 4 digit is mandatory
    d) HSN code 8 digit is mandatory

20. Suppliers liable to be registered where it makes a taxable supply of goods of services if its aggregate turnover in a financial year exceeds ₹:
    a) 7 lakhs
    b) 9 lakhs
    c) 11 lakhs
    d) 13 lakhs

21. Suppliers liable to be registered where it makes a taxable supply of goods of services if its aggregate turnover in a financial year exceeds ₹: (For NE states and Sikkim)
    a) 2 lakhs
    b) 4 lakhs
    c) 6 lakhs
    d) 8 lakhs

22. GST registration fee is Rs.:
    a) 10,000
    b) 20,000
    c) 30,000
    d) Free of cost

23. Penalty for not registering under GST is:
    a) 10% tax or minimum10,000
    b) 10% tax or minimum 20,000
    c) 10% tax or minimum 30,000
    d) 10% tax or minimum 40,000
24. The rate of tax for manufacturer under GST is:
    a) 1%
    b) 2%
    c) 3%
    d) 4%
25. The details regarding the outward supply of goods or services shall be provided in:
    a) Form GSTR 1
    b) Form GSTR 2
    c) Form GSTR 3
    d) Form GSTR 4
26. The details regarding the inward supply of goods or services shall be provided in:
    a) Form GSTR 1
    b) Form GSTR 2
    c) Form GSTR 3
    d) Form GSTR 4
27. The refund shall be claimed through:
    a) Form GSTR 1
    b) Form GSTR 2
    c) Form GSTR 3
    d) Form GSTR 4
28. Any person who occasionally undertakes transactions involving supply of goods or services or both, whether as principal or agent or in any other capacity, but who has no fixed place of business or residence in India
    a) Casual taxable person
    b) Resident taxable person
    c) Non - resident taxable person
    d) Casual exempted person
29. A non-resident taxable person required to filled:
    a) Form GSTR 7
    b) Form GSTR 9
    c) Form GSTR 11
    d) Form GSTR 13
30. Non-resident taxable person intends to extend the period of registration indicated in his application of registration, an application in FORM GST REG-11 shall be submitted electronically through the Common Portal:

a) Form GSTR 7
b) Form GSTR 9
c) Form GSTR 11
d) Form GSTR 13

31. The non-resident taxable person shall furnish a return in:
a) Form GSTR 5
b) Form GSTR 7
c) Form GSTR 9
d) Form GSTR 11

32. The organization must apply for UIN using:
a) Form GSTR 11
b) Form GSTR 13
c) Form GSTR 15
d) Form GSTR 17

33. All persons having GST UIN are required to file a quarterly return using:
a) Form GSTR 11
b) Form GSTR 13
c) Form GSTR 15
d) Form GSTR 17

34. The state code of Maharashtra under GSTIN is:
a) 25
b) 27
c) 29
d) 31

35. As per the 2011 census of India total number of state codes under GSTIN are:
a) 31
b) 33
c) 35
d) 37

36. Every person, other than a non-resident taxable person, a person required to deduct tax at source under section:
a) 51
b) 52
c) 53
d) 54

37. Every person, other than a non-resident taxable person, a person required to collect tax at source under section:
a) 51
b) 52
c) 53

d) 54
38. Application for registration using:
    a) Form GSTR 1
    b) Form GSTR 2
    c) Form GSTR 3
    d) Form GSTR 4
39. The Permanent Account Number shall be validated online by the common portal from the database maintained by:
    a) RBI
    b) CBDT
    c) CBEC
    d) Income tax department
40. application for grant of registration has been approved under rule:
    a) 7
    b) 8
    c) 9
    d) 10
41. Any person having multiple business verticals within a State or a Union territory, requiring a separate registration for any of its business verticals under subsection (2) of section:
    a) 20
    b) 25
    c) 30
    d) 35
42. Cancellation of registration rule is:
    a) 21
    b) 22
    c) 23
    d) 24
43. Application for cancellation of registration:
    a) Form GSTR 13
    b) Form GSTR 14
    c) Form GSTR 15
    d) Form GSTR 16
44. A registered person, whose registration is cancelled by the proper officer on his own motion, may submit an application for revocation of cancellation of registration, in:
    a) Form GSTR 21
    b) Form GSTR 22
    c) Form GSTR 23
    d) Form GSTR 24
45. GST being a tax on the event of:

a) Production
b) Services
c) Purchases
d) Supply

46. Casual taxable persons or non-resident taxable persons have to apply for registration at least _________ days in advance before making any supply.
    a) 3
    b) 5
    c) 7
    d) 9

47. The tax shall be deducted at source at the rate of payment made to the supplier.
    a) 1%
    b) 2%
    c) 3%
    d) 4%

48. The aggregate value of all taxable and non-taxable supplies, exempt supplies and exports of goods and/or services of a person is called as:
    a) Gross turnover
    b) Net turnover
    c) Aggregate turnover
    d) Specific turnover

49. A person who supplies the products out of his cultivation land is called as:
    a) Agriculturist
    b) Sellers
    c) Producers
    d) Marketers

50. The taxpayer who are exempted from GST registration:
    a) Producers
    b) Sellers
    c) Agriculturist
    d) Distributors

Answer Keys:

1	B	11	B	21	B	31	A	41	B
2	D	12	A	22	D	32	B	42	B
3	C	13	C	23	A	33	A	43	D
4	A	14	B	24	A	34	B	44	A
5	B	15	A	25	A	35	C	45	D
6	C	16	A	26	B	36	A	46	B
7	D	17	B	27	C	37	B	47	A
8	B	18	C	28	C	38	A	48	C
9	C	19	D	29	B	39	B	49	A
10	C	20	B	30	C	40	C	50	C

Unit 3

SUPPLY UNDER GST AND VALUATION OF SUPPLY

1) When does liability to pay GST arise in case of supply of goods?
   a) On raising of invoice
   b) At the time of supply of goods
   c) At the time of supply of goods
   d) Earliest of any of above
2) What is date of receipt of payment?
   a) Date of entry in the books
   b) Date of payment credited into bank account
   c) Earlier of (a) and (b)
   d) Date of filing of return
3) The value of supply of goods and services shall be the:
   a) Transaction value
   b) MRP
   c) Market price
   d) None of the above
4) When can be the transaction value be rejected for computation of value of supply:
   a) When the buyer and seller are not related and price is not the sole consideration
   b) When the buyer and seller are related and price is not the sole consideration
   c) It can be never rejected
   d) When the goods are sold at very low margin
5) What deductions are allowed from transactions value?
   a) Discounts mention on invoice
   b) Packaging charges mention of invoice
   c) Any discount paid by customer on behalf of the supplier
   d) Freight charges mention on invoice
6) When does the liability to pay GST arise in case of supply of goods?
   a) On raising of invoice
   b) At the time of supply of goods
   c) On receipt of payment
   d) Earliest of a ,b or c
7) What is time of supply of goods under CGST Act, 2017?
   a) Date of issue of invoice Time and Value of Supply 23 Indirect Taxes Committee
   b) Date of receipt of consideration by the supplier
   c) Date of dispatch of goods
   d) Earlier of (a) & (b)
8) What is time of supply of goods liable to tax under reverse charge mechanism?
   a) Date of receipt of goods
   b) Date on which the payment is made
   c) Date immediately following 30 days from the date of issue of invoice by the supplier
   d) Earlier of a/b/c
9) What is the time of supply of vouchers when the supply with respect to the voucher is identifiable?

a) Date of issue of voucher
b) Date of redemption of voucher
c) Earlier of (a) & (b)
d) (a) & (b) whichever is later

10) What is the time of supply of vouchers when the supply with respect to the voucher is not identifiable?
a) Date of issue of voucher
b) Date of redemption of voucher
c) Earlier of (a) & (b)
d) (a) & (b) whichever is later

11) What is date of receipt of payment?
a) Date of entry in the books
b) Date of payment credited into bank account
c) Earlier of a and b
d) Date of filing of return

12) Mr. A supplies goods worth Rs. 24,300 to Mr. B and issues an invoice dated 25.7.2017 for Rs. 24,300 and Mr. B pays Rs. 25,000 on 30.7.2017 against such supply of goods. The excess Rs. 700 (being less than Rs. 1,000) is adjusted in the next invoice for supply of goods issued on 5.8.2017. Identify the time of supply and value of supply:
a) Rs. 25,000 – 30.7.2017
b) For Rs. 24,300 – 25.7.2017 and for Rs. 700 – 30.7.2017
c) Rs. 25,000 – 25.7.2017
d) For Rs. 24,300 – 25.7.2017 and for Rs. 700 – 5.8.2017

13) What is the time of supply of service if the invoice is issued within 30 days from the date of provision of service?
a) Date of issue of invoice
b) Date on which the supplier receives payment
c) Date of provision of service
d) Earlier of (a) & (b)

14) What is the time of supply of service for the supply of taxable services up to Rs.1000 in excess of the amount indicated in the taxable invoice?
a) At the option of the supplier – Invoice date or Date of receipt of consideration
b) Date of issue of invoice
c) Date of receipt of consideration.
d) Date of entry in books of account

15) How is the date of receipt of consideration by the supplier determined?
a) Date on which the receipt of payment is entered in the books of account
b) Date on which the receipt of payment is credited in the bank account
c) Earlier of (a) & (b)
d) (a) & (b) whichever is later

16) What is the time of supply of service in case of reverse charge mechanism?
a) Date on which payment is made to the supplier Time and Value of Supply 25 Indirect Taxes Committee
b) Date immediately following 60 days from the date of issue of invoice
c) Date of invoice
d) Earlier of (a) & (b)

17) What is the time of supply of service in case an associated enterprise receives services from the service provider located outside India?
   a) Date of entry in the books of account of associated enterprise(recipient)
   b) Date of payment
   c) Earlier of (a) & (b)
   d) Date of entry in the books of the supplier of service
18) What is the time of supply of vouchers when the supply with respect to the voucher is identifiable?
   a) Date of issue of voucher
   b) Date of redemption of voucher
   c) Earlier of (a) & (b)
   d) (a) & (b) whichever is later
19) What is the time of supply of vouchers when the supply with respect to the voucher is not identifiable?
   a) Date of issue of voucher
   b) Date of redemption of voucher
   c) Earlier of (a) & (b)
   d) (a) & (b) whichever is later
20) Value of services rendered is Rs. 1,00,000/. Date of issue of invoice is 5th August 2017.Advance Received is Rs. 25,000/- on 20th July 2017. Balance amount received on 7th August 2017. What is the time of supply for Rs. 1,00,000/-
   a) 5th August 2017 for Rs. 1,00,000/-
   b) 20th July 2017 for Rs. 1,00,000/-
   c) 20th July 2017- Rs. 25,000/- and 5th August 2017 for Rs. 75,000/-
   d) 20th July 2017- Rs. 25,000/- and 7th August 2017 for Rs. 75,000/-
21) What are different types of supplies covered under the scope of Supply?
   a) Supplies made with consideration
   b) Supplies made without consideration
   c) Both of the above
   d) None of the above
22) What are the factors differentiating Composite Supply & Mixed Supply?
   a) Nature of bundling i.e. artificial or natural
   b) Existence of Principal Supply
   c) Both of the above
   d) None of the above
23) What are the taxes levied on an intra-State Supply?
   a) CGST
   b) SGST
   c) CGST and SGST
   d) IGST
24) What is the maximum rate prescribed under CGST?
   a) 12%
   b) 28%
   c) 20%
   d) 18%
25) Who will notify the rate of tax to be levied under CGST?

a) Central Government suo moto
b) State Government suo moto
c) GST Council suo moto
d) Central Government as per the recommendations of the GST Council

26) What are the supplies on which reverse charge mechanism would apply?
a) Notified categories of goods or services or both
b) Inward supply of goods or services or both from an unregistered dealer
c) Both of the above
d) None of the above

27) Which of the following taxes will be levied on Imports?
a) CGST
b) SGST
c) IGST
d) Exempt Levy and Collection of Tax

28) Which of the following taxes would be levied on an intra-State supply of goods or services or both:
a) CGST
b) Union territory tax
c) Both of the above
d) IGST

29) Is there any maximum rate prescribed under UTGST?
a) 14%
b) 28%
c) 20%
d) 30%

30) _____________ supply shall attract IGST?
a) Intra-State
b) Inter-State
c) Both
d) Union territories

31) Is there any ceiling limit prescribed on the rate under IGST?
a) 14%
b) 40%
c) 26%
d) 30%

32) What if an e-commerce operator having no physical presence in the taxable territory, does not have a representative in the taxable territory?
a) His will have to discharge his tax liability in foreign currency
b) He will not be liable to tax
c) He has to appoint a person in the taxable territory for the purpose of paying tax on his behalf
d) None of the above

33) Unless and until notified, IGST shall not be levied on the inter-State supply of which of the following:
a) Industrial alcohol
b) Works contract

c) Petroleum
d) None of the above

34) Which of the following is an inter-State supply?
   a) Supplier of goods located in Delhi and place of supply of goods SEZ located in Delhi
   b) Supplier of goods located in Delhi and place of supply of goods in Jaipur
   c) Supplier of goods located in Delhi and place of supply of goods SEZ located in Chandigarh
   d) All the above

35) Which of the following is an intrastate supply?
   a) Supplier of goods located in Delhi and place of supply of goods SEZ located in Delhi
   b) Supplier of goods located in Delhi and place of supply of goods in Jaipur
   c) Supplier of goods located in Delhi and place of supply of goods in Delhi
   d) All the above

36) Which of the following transaction is inter-state supply of goods involving movement of goods?
   a) Location of supplier is in Bangalore and location of recipient is in Mumbai
   b) Location of supplier is in Bangalore and place of supply is Mumbai
   c) Location of supplier and place of supply is Bangalore
   d) None of the above

37) Supply of goods in the course of import of territory of India is:
   a) Intrastate supply
   b) Inter-State supply
   c) Export
   d) Inter-state trade or commerce

38) Which of the following supply involving movement of goods is an intra-State supply?
   a) Location of supplier in Kerala and place of supply in Tamil Nadu
   b) Location of supplier in Karnataka and place of supply in Karnataka
   c) Location of supplier in Kerala and place of supply on Andhra Pradesh
   d) None of the above

39) Place of supply in case of installation of elevator is:
   a) Where the movement of elevator commences from the supplier's place
   b) Where the delivery of elevator is taken
   c) Where the installation of elevator is made
   d) Where address of the recipient is mentioned in the invoice

40) Place of supply of food taken onboard at Delhi for an aircraft departing from Delhi to Bangalore via Hyderabad is:
   a) Address of the aircraft carrier mentioned on the invoice of the supplier
   b) Delhi
   c) Jaipur
   d) Hyderabad

41) In case of any ambiguity where place of supply of goods cannot be determined as provided in IGST Act, 2106 who will determine the place of supply?
   a) Central Government on recommendation of the Council
   b) State and Central Government on recommendation of the Council
   c) Central Government
   d) In a manner as may be prescribed

42) What is location of supply in case of importation of goods?
   a) Customs port where the goods are cleared
   b) Location of the importer
   c) Place where the goods are delivered after clearance from customs port
   d) Owner of the goods
43) Real estate agent in Delhi charges brokerage fee to Company A located in Chandigarh for assistance in getting a commercial property in Kolkata. Which is the place of supply in this case?
   a) Delhi
   b) Mumbai
   c) Chandigarh
   d) Kolkata
44) Mr. X a resident from Pune conducts training for employees of P Ltd. being a registered person under GST based out in Chennai at a resort in Darjeeling. The place of supply in this case is:
   a) Chennai
   b) Pune
   c) Darjeeling
   d) Mumbai
45) Place of supply of service for DTH by ABC Pvt. Ltd. located in Mumbai to customer in Patna is:
   a) Mumbai
   b) Delhi
   c) Kolkata
   d) Patna
46) Mr. X of Hyderabad not having bank account takes a demand draft in Kolkata from ABC Bank for his visa purpose. The place of supply is:
   a) Hyderabad
   b) Mumbai
   c) Delhi
   d) Kolkata
47) The provider of AMC service outside India has entered into an agreement for an aircraft company PQR located in India AMC. The service provider provides repair service to the aircraft when it was in India. The place of service in this case is:
   a) Outside India
   b) Mumbai
   c) Delhi
   d) India
48) If XYZ Ltd a company based out of Bangalore, awards online maintenance contract of its servers located in Mumbai office to Y INC, a company based out of USA, and as per the terms of the online maintenance X INC shall be required to perform regular maintenance from USA using Internet, then the place of supply is:
   a) Bangalore
   b) Mumbai
   c) USA
   d) UK

49) Mr. Y residing in Ahmedabad appoints an architect in Delhi to provide Indian traditional
home design for his proposed construction at Los Angeles, the place of supply of service is:
a) Los Angeles
b) Ahmedabad
c) Delhi
d) Chennai
50) If NM shipping Co. located in Chennai charges ocean freight charges for transport of goods
to California for a customer located in Bangalore, the place of supply of service will be:
a) Chennai
b) California
c) Bangalore
d) Kolkata

Answer Keys:

1	D	11	C	21	C	31	B	41	D
2	C	12	D	22	C	32	C	42	B
3	A	13	B	23	C	33	C	43	D
4	B	14	A	24	C	34	D	44	A
5	A	15	C	25	D	35	C	45	D
6	D	16	D	26	C	36	B	46	D
7	D	17	C	27	C	37	D	47	D
8	D	18	A	28	C	38	B	48	B
9	A	19	B	29	C	39	C	49	A
10	B	20	C	30	B	40	B	50	B

Unit 4

INPUT TAX CREDIT UNDER GST & RETURNS

1) Whether definition of Inputs includes capital goods:
   a) Yes
   b) No
   c) Certain capital goods only
   d) None of the above
2) Is it mandatory to capitalize the capital goods in books of Accounts?
   a) Yes
   b) No
   c) Optional
   d) None of the above
3) Whether credit on capital goods can be taken immediately on receipt of the goods?
   a) Yes
   b) No
   c) After usage of such capital goods
   d) After capitalizing in books of Accounts
4) Whether it is necessary to capitalize the capital goods in the books of account:
   a) Yes
   b) No
   c) Only use of goods is recognized
   d) Accounting is not relevant Input Tax Credit
5) The term "used in the course or furtherance of business" means?
   a) It should be directly co related to output supply
   b) It is planned to use in the course of business
   c) It is used in the course of business
   d) It is used in the course of business for making outward supply
6) Under section 16(2) of CGST Act how many conditions are to be fulfilled for the entitlement of credit?
   a) All the conditions
   b) Any two conditions
   c) Conditions not specified
   d) None of the above
7) Whether credit on inputs should be availed based on receipt of documents or receipt of goods:
   a) Receipt of goods
   b) Receipt of Documents
   c) Both
   d) Either receipt of documents or Receipt of goods
8) In case supplier has deposited the taxes but the receiver has not received the documents, is receiver entitled to avail credit?
   a) Yes it will be auto populated in recipient monthly returns
   b) No as one of the conditions of 16(2) is not fulfilled
   c) Yes if the receiver can prove later that documents are received subsequently

d) None of the above
9) Input tax credit on capital goods and Inputs can be availed in one installment or in multiple installments?
   a) In thirty six installments
   b) In twelve installments
   c) In one installment
   d) In six installments
10) The tax-paying documents in section 16(2) is:
   a) Bill of entry, Invoice raised on RCM supplies, etc.
   b) Acknowledged copy of tax paid to department
   c) Supply invoice by the recipient
   d) Any of the above
11) The time limit to pay the value of supply with taxes to avail the input tax credit?
   a) Three months
   b) Six Months
   c) One hundred and eighty days
   d) Till the date of filing of Annual Return
12) Can the recipient avail the Input tax credit for the part payment of the amount to the supplier within one hundred and eighty days?
   a) Yes on full tax amount and partly value amount
   b) No he can't until full amount is paid to supplier
   c) Yes but proportionately to the extent of value and tax paid Input Tax Credit
   d) Not applicable
13) Whether credit can be availed without actual receipt of goods where goods are transferred through transfer of document of title before or during the movement of goods?
   a) Yes
   b) No
   c) Yes, in specific instances
   d) Can be availed only after transfer of document of title after movement of goods
14) Whether depreciation on tax component of capital goods and Plant and Machinery and whether input tax credit is Permissible?
   a) Yes
   b) No
   c) Input tax credit is eligible if depreciation on tax component is not availed
   d) None of the above
15) What is the maximum time limit to claim the Input tax credit?
   a) Till the date of filing annual return
   b) Due date of September month which is following the financial year
   c) Earliest of (a) or (b)
   d) Later of (a) or (b)
16) Proportionate credit for capital goods is allowed:
   a) For business and non-business purpose
   b) For business or non- business purpose
   c) Both of the above
   d) None of the above
17) Banking company or Financial Institution have an option of claiming:

a) Eligible Credit or 50% credit
b) Only 50% Credit
c) Only Eligible credit
d) Eligible credit and 50% credit

18) Can Banking Company or Financial Institution withdraw the option of availing actual credit or 50% credit anytime in the financial year?
a) Yes
b) No
c) Yes with permission of Authorized officer
d) Not applicable

19) Any input tax paid on purchase of goods or services by an assessee for employees is eligible?
a) No
b) Yes
c) Yes, on the services notified which are obligatory for an employer to provide to its employees under any law for the time being in force
d) Not applicable

20) A supplier of goods or services pays tax under under section 74,129 and 130 (fraud, willful misstatement etc.). Receiver of goods can avail its credit:
a) Yes
b) No
c) Yes, after receipt of goods or services
d) Yes, after receipt of invoice for goods or services

21) An assessee obtains new registration, voluntary registration, change of scheme from composition to regular scheme and from exempted goods/services to taxable goods/services. It can avail credit on inputs lying in stock. What is the time limit for taking said credit:
a) 1 year from the date of invoice
b) 3 year from the date of invoice
c) 5 year from the date of invoice
d) None of the above

22) Credit on Input services or capital goods held in stock can be availed in case of new Registration/Voluntary Registration:
a) Yes
b) No
c) Yes on Input services only
d) Yes on capital goods only

23) Eligibility of credit on capital goods in case of change of scheme from Composition scheme to Regular scheme:
a) Eligible during application for Regular scheme
b) Not eligible
c) Yes, Immediately before the date from which he becomes liable to pay tax under the Regular scheme
d) None of the above

24) Can the unutilized input tax credit be transferred in case of change in constitution of business?
a) Not possible
b) No, it will be exhausted

c) Yes, It will be transferred only if there is provision for transfer of liabilities
d) It will be transferred only if it is shown in books of Accounts of transferor

25) Is Input tax fully restricted in case of switchover from taxable to exempt supplies:
a) Yes
b) No
c) Proportionately restricted
d) Not restricted

26) Is Input tax to be paid in case of switchover from taxable to exempt supplies:
a) Yes, equivalent to the credit in respect of inputs held in stock and on capital goods held in stock
b) No
c) Yes full credit
d) No should be debited to electronic credit ledger

27) Is Input tax to be reversed in case of supply of capital goods:
a) Yes fully
b) No
c) Yes, to extent of credit taken as reduced by prescribed percentage or tax on transaction value whichever is higher
d) Yes to the extent of transaction value of such goods

28) The time limit beyond which if goods are not returned, the inputs sent for job work shall be treated as supply:
a) One year
b) Five years
c) Six months
d) Seven years

29) The time limit beyond which if goods are not returned, the capital goods sent for job work shall be treated as supply:
a) One year
b) Five years
c) Three Years
d) Seven years

30) Principal entitled for input tax credit on inputs sent for job work:
a) If goods sent are returned within one year
b) If goods sent are returned within three years
c) If goods sent are returned within six months
d) If goods sent are returned within nine months

31) Principal entitled for input tax credit on capital goods if sent for job work:
a) If goods sent are returned within one year
b) If goods sent are returned within three years
c) If goods sent are returned within six months
d) If goods sent are returned within nine months

32) Is the principal entitled for credit of goods though he has not received the goods and has been sent to job worker directly by vendor:
a) Yes
b) No
c) Yes vendor should be located in same place

    d) None of the above
33) In case of ISD whether distributor and recipient should have same PAN:
    a) Yes
    b) No
    c) Yes if in same state and different in other state
    d) None of the above
34) Can the credit distributed by an ISD exceed the amount available for distribution:
    a) Yes
    b) No
    c) Partly correct
    d) None of the above
35) If credit applicable to more than one recipient, then it shall be distributed:
    a) Equally
    b) On Pro rata basis to the aggregate turnover of such recipients
    c) Proportionately
    d) As per Adhoc Ratio
36) The credit attributable to a particular recipient shall be distributed to:
    a) Only to that recipient
    b) To all the recipients
    c) To few recipients
    d) None of the recipients
37) A person is entitled to take credit of input tax as self-assessed in the return and credited to Electronic credit ledger on:
    a) Final basis
    b) Provisional basis
    c) Partly Provisional and partly final basis
    d) None of the above
38) Provisional Input tax credit can be utilized against:
    a) Any Tax liability
    b) Self Assessed output Tax liability
    c) Interest and Penalty
    d) Fine
39) Matching of Input Tax credit on inward supply by recipient is undertaken with:
    a) Monthly return filed by the supplier
    b) Outward supply filed by the supplier
    c) Invoices maintained by the supplier
    d) None of the above
40) Is it mandatory that the tax on the supply has to be paid by the supplier so that the recipient can claim credit?
    a) No
    b) Yes
    c) Optional
    d) Not Applicable
41) If there is Mis-match of supplier's outward supply and recipient's claim for Input Tax credit on the same transaction:
    a) It shall be added as output tax liability in the hands of receiver

b) It shall be reduced as output tax liability in the hands of receiver
c) It shall be increased as input tax credit in the hands of receiver
d) It shall be deceased as input tax credit in the hands of supplier

42) Input Tax credit as credited in Electronic Credit ledger can be utilized for:
a) Payment of Interest
b) Payment of penalty
c) Payment of Fine
d) Payment of Taxes

43) The details of outward supplies of goods or services shall be submitted by:
a) 10th of the succeeding month
b) 18th of the succeeding month
c) 15th of the succeeding month
d) 20th of the succeeding month

44) Details of Outward supplies shall include:
a) Invoice
b) Credit and Debit notes
c) Revised invoice issued in relation to outward supplies
d) All the above

45) The details submitted by the outward supplier in Form GSTR 1 shall be furnished to the recipient regular dealer in form:
a) GSTR 4A
b) GSTR 5A
c) GSTR 2A
d) GSTR 6A

46) The details submitted by the outward supplier in Form GSTR 1 shall be furnished to the recipient compounding dealer in form:
a) GSTR 4A
b) GSTR 5A
c) GSTR 2A
d) GSTR 6A

47) The details submitted by the outward supplier in Form GSTR 1 shall be furnished to the input service distributor in form:
a) GSTR 4A
b) GSTR 5A
c) GSTR 2A
d) GSTR 6A

48) Details of Inward supplies shall include:
a) Inward supplies of goods and services communicated in Form GSTR 2A
b) Inward supplies in respect of which tax is payable under reverse charge mechanism
c) Inward supplies of goods and services not declared by suppliers
d) All the above

49) Any modification / deletion done by the recipient to the details contained in Form GSTR 2 shall be communicated to the supplier in:
a) Form GSTR 1A
b) Form GSTR 3A
c) Form GSTR 6A

d) Form GSTR 2A

50) The supplier on receiving the communication in Form GSTR 1A shall accept, reject or modify the details by:
   a) 18th of the succeeding month
   b) 20th of the month succeeding the quarter
   c) 17th of the succeeding month
   a) 10th of the succeeding month

51) Every registered taxable person shall be entitled to take credit of input tax in his return and such input tax credit shall be credited to:
   a) Personal Ledger Account
   b) Refund account
   c) Electronic Cash Ledger
   d) Electronic Credit Ledger

52) The details of every credit note relating to outward supplies furnished by the registered taxable person shall be matched:
   a) With corresponding reduction in claim for input tax credit by the corresponding taxable person in his valid return for the same tax period or any subsequent tax period.
   b) For duplication of claims for reduction in the output tax liability
   c) All of the above
   d) None of the above

53) Every registered taxable person who is required to get his accounts audited under section 35(5) shall furnish electronically:
   a) Annual return
   b) Audited copy of annual accounts
   c) Reconciliation statement reconciling the value of supplies declared in the return and the financial statement
   d) All of the above

54) The annual return shall be filed by the registered taxable person in form:
   a) GSTR 7
   b) GSTR 9
   c) GSTR 9A
   d) GSTR 10

55) Find the correct match of annual returns to be filed:
   a) Registered taxable person – Form GSTR 8
   b) Input service distributor – Form GSTR 9
   c) Non Resident taxable person – Form GSTR 9B
   d) Compounding taxable person – Form GSTR 9A

56) Notice to non-filers of return shall be sent in Form:
   a) GSTR 5
   b) GSTR 3
   c) GSTR 3A
   d) GSTR 10

57) Any registered taxable person who fails to furnish the details and file the return within the due date prescribed shall be liable to:
   a) Interest at the rate of 1% per month
   b) Late fee of Rs. 100 for every day up to Rs. 5000

c) Both (a) and (b)
d) None of the above

58) Which of the following is correct?
   a) Failure to file annual return within due date attracts a late fee of Rs. 100 per day up to 0.25% of his turnover
   b) Failure to file annual return within due date attracts late fee of 1% of his turnover till the failure continues
   c) Failure to file annual returns within due date attracts a late fee of Rs. 100 per day up to 1% of his turnover.
   d) On failure to file annual return within due date the proper officer shall issue a notice of non-filing on such person

59) A goods and service tax practitioner can undertake the following activities if authorized by the taxable person:
   a) Furnish details inward and outward supplies
   b) Furnish monthly / quarterly return
   c) Furnish Annual and Final return
   d) All of the above

60) Refunds will not be allowed in cases of:
   a) Exports made on payment of tax
   b) Exports made without payment of tax
   c) Inverted duty structures where tax on inputs are higher than tax on outputs
   d) All of the above

61) Refund application is to be filed before the expiry of _____________ from the relevant date.
   a) Two years
   b) One year
   c) 180 days
   d) 260 days

62) A specialized agency of the UNO can claim refund of tax paid on:
   a) Intra-State supply of goods and/or services
   b) Inter-state supply of goods and/or services
   c) Inward supply of goods and/or services
   d) All of the above

63) The applicant is not required to furnish documentary evidence if the amount of refund claimed is less than:
   a) Rs 6 lakhs
   b) Rs 2 lakhs
   c) Rs 10 lakhs
   d) Rs 20 lakhs

64) Refund shall not be paid to the applicant if the amount of refund is less than:
   a) Rs 1000
   b) Rs 5000
   c) Rs 7000
   d) Rs 10000

65) The sanction refund amount can be adjusted against the payments which he is liable to pay but remains unpaid under the earlier law.
   a) Tax

b) Penalty
c) Interest and other amounts
d) All of the above

66) The time limit to proper officer to pass final order after accepting the refund application is:
a) Within sixty days from the date of receipt of application
b) Within eighty days from the date of receipt of application
c) Within ninety days from the date of receipt of application
d) Within thirty days from the date of receipt of application

67) Interest on refund amount is required to be paid after expiry of ………. from the date of receipt of the application.
a) 60 days
b) 90 days
c) 180 days
d) 240 days

68) What is the rate of interest to be payable in case of delay in sanctioning the refund claimed:
a) Not exceeding 6%
b) Not exceeding 8%
c) Not exceeding 10%
d) Not exceeding 12%

69) The Tourist can claim Refund of following taxes paid:
a) CGST and SGST/UTGST on supply of Goods and services
b) IGST on supply of goods consumed in Jammu & Kashmir
c) Tax paid on the supply of scotch to be taken out of India
d) None of the above

70) Tourist means a person:
a) Not normally resident in India
b) Stays for less than 200 days in India
c) Stays for legitimate and Non-Immigrant purpose
d) Both (a) and (b)

Answer Keys:

1	A	11	C	21	A	31	B	41	A	51	D	61	A
2	A	12	B	22	B	32	A	42	D	52	C	62	C
3	A	13	C	23	C	33	A	43	A	53	D	63	B
4	A	14	C	24	C	34	B	44	D	54	B	64	A
5	C	15	C	25	A	35	B	45	C	55	D	65	D
6	A	16	A	26	A	36	A	46	A	56	C	66	A
7	B	17	A	27	C	37	B	47	D	57	B	67	A
8	B	18	B	28	A	38	B	48	D	58	A	68	A
9	C	19	C	29	C	39	B	49	A	59	D	69	D
10	A	20	A	30	A	40	B	50	C	60	A	70	D

Unit 5

CUSTOM DUTY AND INDIRECT TAXATION

1) Which of the following commodities is not subjected to payment of Export Duty at the time of export?
   a) Iron Ore Pallets
   b) Bauxite (natural) Calcined
   c) Snake skin
   d) Ferrous Waste and Scrap
2) What is the time limit prescribed under the Customs Act, 2016 as on date for issuance of demand notice U/s 28 of the Customs Act, 1962 in cases where fraud, suppression of facts, willful mis-statement is not involved?
   a) Six months
   b) One year
   c) Two Years
   d) Three Years
3) Which of the following Rules have been substituted with new Rules w.e.f. 01.04.2016?
   a) Customs (Import of Goods at Concessional Rate of Duty for Manufacture of Excisable Goods) Rules, 1996
   b) Customs Valuation (Determination of Value of Imported Goods) Rules, 2007.
   c) Customs, Central Excise Duties and Service Tax Drawback Rules, 1995.
   d) Foreign Privileged Persons (Regulation of Customs Privileges) Rules, 1957.
4) What is the quantum of pre deposit for a person filing second appeal before CESTAT when 7.5% of the duty has already been pre deposited by him at the time of filing first appeal before Commissions (Appeals)?
   a) 10% of duty.
   b) 5% of duty
   c) 2.5 % of duty
   d) NIL
5) A person can make an application to the settlement commission under Custom Act?
   a) Before issue of show cause notice.
   b) Before adjudication.
   c) Within thirty days from the date of issue of O-I-O.
   d) Before filing appeal.
6) Which of these is/are not an adjudicating authority under Customs Act, 1962?
   a) Commissioner of Customs
   b) Principal Commissioner of Customs
   c) Commissioner (Appeals) & Tribunal
   d) Assistant Commissioner of Customs
7) As per section 11 of the Customs Act, 1962, which of these is a purpose for which Central Government may prohibit (absolutely or conditionally) the importation / exportation of any specified goods?
   a) The prevention of smuggling
   b) The conservation of foreign exchange and the safeguarding of balance of payments
   c) The protection of patents, trademarks, copyrights, designs and geographical indications

d) All of the above
8) Which section of the Customs Act, 1962 provides for levy of Customs duty on import and export of goods?
   a) Section 3
   b) Section 12
   c) Section 14
   d) Section 28
9) Where shall an appeal against the Order passed by the CESTAT relating to the valuation of goods shall lie?
   a) High Court
   b) Supreme Court
   c) Central Government
   d) CESTAT cannot pass an order on valuation matters
10) Under Section 14 of the Customs Act 1962, the transaction value shall be calculated with reference to the rate of exchange as in force on the date on which:
   a) Date of Invoice
   b) The date of issuance of the Bill of lading
   c) Date of filing IGM
   d) Date of filing the Bill of Entry
11) As on date, the On-Site Post Clearance Audit (OSPCA) has been made operational by the Board for:
   a) ACP clients
   b) AEO clients
   c) All the manufacturer-importers with Customs duty payments in excess of Rs.1 Cr per annum
   d) All importers and exporters
12) Under what situation, SCN transferred to the call book can be taken out of call book?
   a) When the grounds on basis of which a SCN has been transferred to call book, ceases to exist.
   b) It depends upon the overall pendency position of SCNs in the Commissionerate.
   c) SCN can be kept in the call book for five years.
   d) SCN, when transferred to call book, cannot be taken out of call book any point of time.
13) What is the quantum of pre-deposit for the Department at the time of filing application (appeal) (w. e. f. 06.08.2014) before the Commissioner (Appeals):-
   a) 5% of the duty, in case where duty or duty and penalty are in dispute; or penalty, where such penalty is in dispute (aggregate of all penalties imposed)
   b) 7.5% of the duty, in case where duty or duty and penalty are in dispute; or penalty, where such penalty is in dispute (aggregate of all penalties imposed)
   c) 10% of the duty, in case where duty or duty and penalty are in dispute; or penalty, where such penalty is in dispute (aggregate of all penalties impo sed)
   d) Nil
14) Export Income earned by which of the following type of manufacturing Unit is normally eligible for exemption from payment of Income Tax under the Income Tax Act, 1961?
   a) Export Oriented Unit
   b) Jewellery manufacturing Unit in DTA
   c) SEZ unit

d) Garment Manufacturing Unit

15) Under which of the following Export Promotion Schemes, Capital Goods are allowed to be imported duty free?
a) Export Promotion Capital goods scheme
b) Software Technology Park Scheme
c) Special Economic Zone Scheme
d) All of the above

16) Indirect taxes are taxes on________
a) Consumption
b) Distribution
c) Proportion
d) Progression

17) Central Excise Act was passed in the year________
a) 1914
b) 1924
c) 1934
d) 1944

18) The amount payable to the dealer as a sale consideration is __________
a) Sale price
b) Sales tax
c) Sales duty
d) Sales turnover

19) A sale of goods with no tax payable is __________
a) Zero sale
b) Zero tax
c) Zero rate sale
d) Zero turnover

20) Union list consists of ______ entries.
a) 77
b) 87
c) 97
d) 107

21) Levy of tax on Sale of Goods specified in______
a) Section 2
b) Section 3
c) Section 4
d) Section 5

22) Tax levy on Sugarcane is specified in________
a) Section 9
b) Section 10
c) Section 11
d) Section 12

23) Purchase tax levy is specified in __________
a) Section 11
b) Section 12
c) Section 13

d) Section 14
24) Article ______________ of the constitution has laid down the levy and collection.
   a) 263
   b) 264
   c) 265
   d) 266
25) Government from time to time fixes tariff value which is called ____________ Value.
   a) Transaction
   b) Tariff
   c) Notional
   d) Rational
26) ______ is the duty levied on commodity produced within the country for sale within the country.
   a) Sales Duty
   b) Customs Duty
   c) Import Duty
   d) Excise Duty
27) ----------- means the time at which the goods cleared from the factory.
   a) Time of removal
   b) Time of resale
   c) Time of reuse
   d) Time of re engineering
28) A customs valuation rule was imposed in the year.
   a) 1985
   b) 1986
   c) 1987
   d) 1988
29) Customs and central excise rules was passed in the year.
   a) 1992
   b) 1993
   c) 1994
   d) 1995
30) ------------ means goods transported by vessel.
   a) Government goods
   b) Railway goods
   c) Coastal goods
   d) Passenger goods
31) ----------------- are goods which are chargeable to duty.
   a) Capital goods
   b) Exciseable goods
   c) Chargeable goods
   d) Dutiable goods
32) ------------ is a tax levied for the special purpose.
   a) Surcharge
   b) CESS
   c) Toll tax

Answer Keys:

1	A	11	A	21	B	31	D	41	A
2	C	12	A	22	C	32	B	42	A
3	A	13	D	23	B	33	A	43	A
4	C	14	C	24	C	34	A	44	A
5	B	15	D	25	C	35	B	45	A
6	C	16	A	26	D	36	A	46	A
7	D	17	D	27	A	37	A	47	B
8	B	18	A	28	D	38	D	48	A
9	B	19	C	29	D	39	A	49	B
10	D	20	C	30	C	40	A	50	A

42) Captively consumed goods means ------------
   a) Goods manufactured and consumed within the factory
   b) Goods manufactured
   c) Goods purchased
   d) Goods received from the branch
43) If a tax is based on the sale price of the product it is:
   a) Cascading effect
   b) VAT
   c) Rebate of tax
   d) Refund of tax
44) Excise duty should be levied on ---------- purposes.
   a) Revenue
   b) Expenditure
   c) Maintenance
   d) Savings
45) A person who neither intends to hold nor holds any title to the goods or services is called?
   a) Pure Agent
   b) Dealer
   c) Service tax provider
   d) Manufacturer
46) Under Invoice method, tax credit can't be claimed unless and until the --------------
   a) Tax Invoice is produced
   b) Tax amount paid
   c) Goods are delivered
   d) Actual sales take place
47) CHA stands for:
   a) Clearing house agents
   b) Customs house agents
   c) Central home agents
   d) Central clearing house agents
48) -------------- means area of customs station.
   a) Customs area
   b) Clearing area
   c) Conveyance area
   d) Coastal area
49) CVD stands for:
   a) Conditional duty
   b) Countervailing duty
   c) Customs value duty
   d) Central value duty
50) Which of the following duties are under the purview of the state?
   a) VAT
   b) Central Excise duty
   c) Customs duty
   d) Service tax

d) OCTROI

33) ------------ is a tax on using a bridge or a road.
   a) Toll tax
   b) Toll gate duty
   c) Toll fee
   d) Toll duty

34) Apex body for administering indirect taxes is:
   a) Central Board of Excise and Customs
   b) Chief Commissioner of Income Taxes
   c) Central Board of Direct Taxes
   d) Chief Commissioner of Central Excise

35) The tax reduces the taxpayers burden on purchasing is ----------
   a) Expense effect
   b) Income effect
   c) Price effect
   d) Substitution effect

36) Essential for a valid sale requires:
   a) Transfer of goods
   b) Production of goods
   c) Storage of goods
   d) Inspection of goods

37) No rebate is allowed if the rebate amount is less than:
   a) Rs. 500
   b) Rs. 1,000
   c) Rs. 1,500
   d) Rs. 2,000

38) The unutilized CENVAT Credit can be carried forward upto:
   a) 6 months
   b) 8 years
   c) 10 years
   d) Without any time limit

39) CENVAT Credit on inputs other than capital goods can be allowed at:
   a) A. 100%
   b) B. 50%
   c) C. 25%
   d) D. 0%

40) Registration is not required if the turnover for SSI units is -----------
   a) Less than 15 lakhs
   b) Less than 90 lakhs
   c) Less than 100 lakhs
   d) Less than 110 lakhs

41) The period covered by the return is called a Tax period and will cover a __________
   a) Calendar month
   b) Calendar year
   c) Half a month
   d) Six month